GRITS

God Reigns In The Soul

For Joy, Libby & CeCe -
This little book is a treasury
of wisdom - and I pray
it will bless you as it has me -
With all Love,
ZaZa - ♡

Pam Morris Hanckel

ISBN 978-1-63844-106-9 (paperback)
ISBN 978-1-63844-107-6 (digital)

Christian Faith Publishing, Inc.
832 Park Avenue
Meadville, PA 16335
www.christianfaithpublishing.com

Printed in the United States of America

To the memory of my parents. Their love for each other was amazing, beautiful, and incredible, and they taught me the true meaning of life and love.

My daddy was my fishing buddy, my hunting partner, my friend, my mentor, and most of all, my father. His lessons were taught to me through his actions, needing very few words. He taught me about caring for others through his unselfish giving to those in need. He always put others' needs above his own. His contagious smile and kindness were shared with all he met. His humility was a true tribute to the awesome person he was. His handshake was his word. The experiences we shared in the woods, rivers, and oceans taught me a deep love and respect for life and nature. He was the anchor of our family.

My mom was not only my mother but my friend, and was always there to encourage me in everything I attempted. She laughed when I laughed and cried when I cried and was always by my side to support me. She had a beautiful smile and personality, and all who knew her loved her. She would make the whole room light up and laugh with her entertaining jokes.

My parents' lives reflected the kind of life Jesus would want us to live. They were full of faith, love, joy, and kindness. My deep faith arose from observing the lives that they led and the values that they taught me. I can never thank my heavenly Father enough for giving me the most wonderful earthly mother and father a girl could ever have. I will always cherish my memories of our time together and will love them forever. Many of the stories in this book reflect some of the wonderful times we had together.

Acknowledgment

I would also like to acknowledge my dear friend Beth Renken who helped make this book possible. We met in college, became friends, married best friends, and raised our families together here in Charleston. It is amazing how our lives have mirrored each other's throughout the years, and she has become more like a sister than a friend.

I remember my school days, and English was not my subject. I still remember the familiar words from my teachers, "Content good, but grammar needs a lot of help." And through the years, things have not changed.

Why God chose me to write a book is beyond my understanding, but He did, and then He blessed me with Beth, my wonderful friend who has worked with me to correct every grammar, spelling, and verb-tense issue and helped me make each story come alive. I can never thank her enough for the many hours she worked helping me piece this book together and for encouraging me every step of the way.

God had a plan bringing us together so many years ago, and I am forever grateful for her love and friendship and the faith we share.

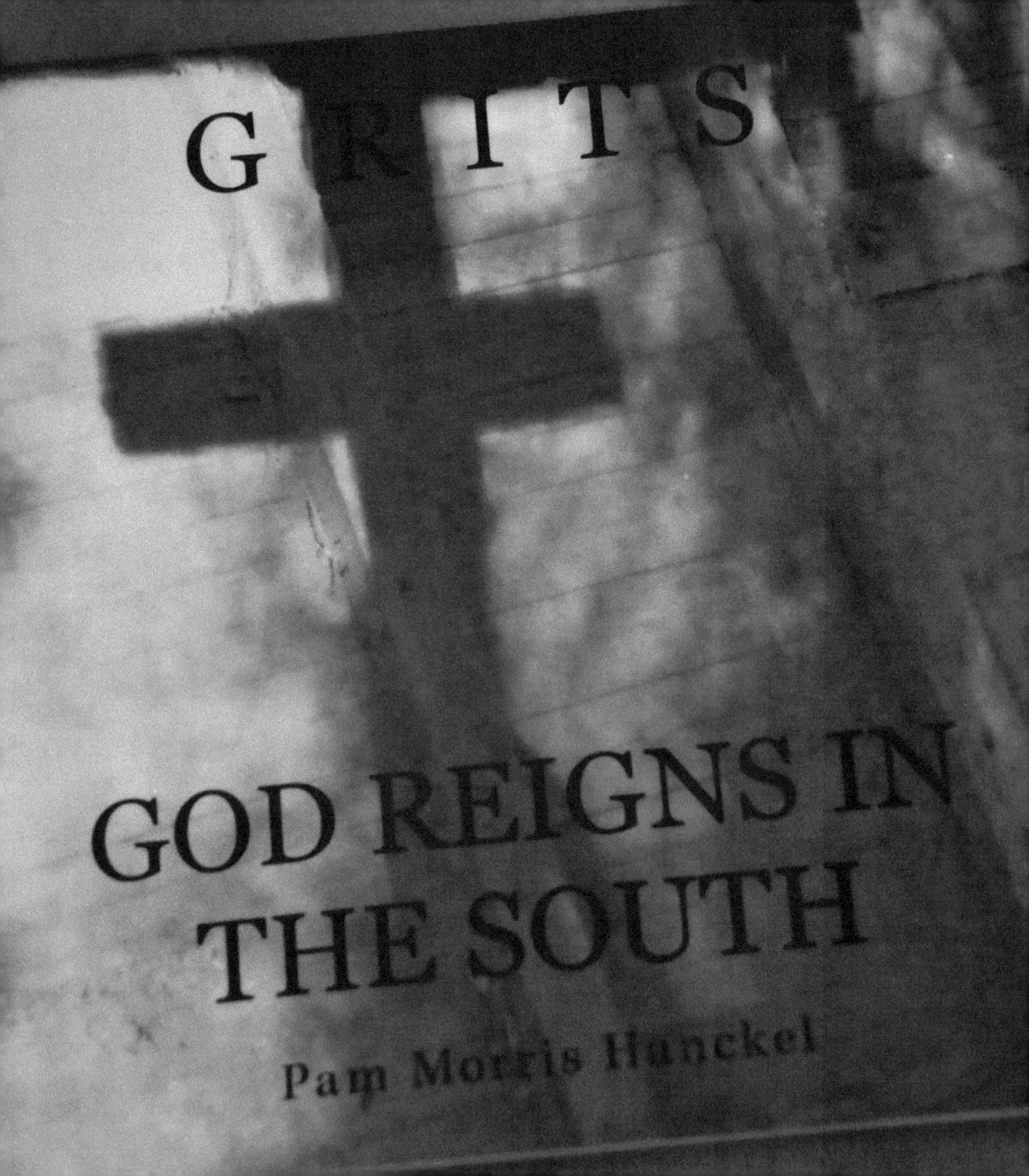
G R I T S
GOD REIGNS IN THE SOUTH
Pam Morris Hunckel

My Fifty-Year Project

I was raised by loving parents who taught me at an early age the importance of faith and trust in God. They took me to church, read me Bible stories, and taught me about the power of prayer. And I am so glad they did.

In the early 1960s, when I was about eight years old, I overheard my parents talking about the threat of war, building fallout shelters to hide in, and the possibility of my father and brothers going to war. I was terrified. I can vividly remember running to my room and grabbing my Bible. I could hear my Sunday School teacher telling us if we were ever afraid, we needed to read our Bible and pray to God for help, so that's just what I did.

As I read, the little bit I could read at that age, I felt God telling me I had to tell others to read their Bibles and pray. So on torn-up pieces of notebook paper, in pencil, I printed, "READ YOUR BIBLES, LOVE YOUR NEIGHBOR, AND PRAY FOR PEACE."

At eight years old, I doubt all of it was spelled correctly, but I felt much better and knew this was what I needed to do. The next day I secretly put the notes in our neighbors' mailboxes. I walked the long road back to my house, and I felt a peace I did not understand, but I knew everything was going to be just fine. I knew without a doubt that God would answer my prayers. I never told anyone what I had done, but I continued praying and reading my Bible, and I was no longer afraid. God provided a peace within me, and my worst fears never happened.

As I grew up, I remained a Christian, straying at times but always coming home to my roots. For years I had wanted to make a difference in people's lives. I wanted a purpose. I always remembered what God had done for me as a child and wanted to show my gratitude to Him somehow. I gave to charities and volunteered where I could, but because I was raising three children and working two jobs to make ends meet, there was never enough time or money for me to feel I had really made a difference. God had been so good to me, and I still had that urge to do more for Him. I kept praying.

We eventually opened a family boating business, and soon things began to get better. I now had a little more time and money to contribute to others, and I hoped that this would fulfill my desire to please God. But I still did not feel like I was doing enough.

My children were soon grown and had children of their own. God seemed to be urging me to make sure their faith continued to grow. With their busy schedules, school, sports, birthday parties, and so much more, it was hard for them to attend church regularly or even read any type of devotion. So I decided to write devotions and email to them a few times each week. I kept them short and simple and signed each one "Love, Grits," the name my grandchildren call me.

Then the recession hit, and the economy took a dive. Our boating business was hit hard, and things were falling apart fast. I would lie in bed in a sweat wondering how we could survive because we had put every dime we had into the business. We could lose everything—our home, our business. What had happened to my perfect life?

That same terrified feeling from my childhood returned. I kept reading and praying and continued to write my devotions. My purpose in the devotions was to strengthen the faith of my children, but amazingly the devotions were also strengthening my own faith. I was praying so hard for business success, but maybe God had other plans for me. I could not live with the constant fear, so I finally took the advice of my own devotions and put everything in His hands. I prayed for His will, not mine. I always had faith and trust, but now I needed that pure faith of a child. The faith I had so many years ago. I finally gave it all to God and felt His peace.

For Christmas that year, I compiled all of my devotions into a book and added some photographs I had taken. It was amazing how perfectly the photographs complemented my devotions. When I realized that my name *Grits* stood for "God Reigns In The South," through divine intervention I believe, I had my title. Money was tight, so I only printed enough copies to give to my family and a few close friends, and they all loved them. I got many requests for more copies, but I resisted taking the scary-and-risky step of actually publishing my book.

Finally, after much prayer, I decided to publish my book! I reluctantly maxed out all of my credit cards to place the 1,500 book minimum order. How would I ever sell them all and recover my investment?

It was not easy. Between my two jobs, I would visit retailers asking them to read my book and then let me know if they would like to sell it in their stores. Most of the responses were wonderful, although some rejected it due to the religious content. I learned to deal with rejection and to appreciate acceptance. I thought of Jesus, who was rejected by many but kept going, kept knocking on doors: and so did I. In just three months, every book was sold!

Shortly thereafter, I began to receive the most beautiful letters and emails from friends, as well as complete strangers, telling me how this book had touched their hearts, inspired them, helped them overcome hardships, and had given them peace. I realized that if this book has the potential to touch hearts and bring people closer to God, then I had to continue. This must be my purpose in life. I ordered more books.

It just amazes me that God planted the seed for this project over fifty years ago when he led me as a child to put His message in those mailboxes. I am convinced now that His purpose for me all along was to continue spreading, through my books, the instructions He has given to me: read your Bible, pray, and love one another. It took me a while to understand His plan for me, but His timing was perfect.

This second book, *Grits, God Reigns In The Soul*, is just another step toward fulfilling the purpose God has given me. With COVID-19 and riots and hostility everywhere, I still have God's peace and know His purpose for me. I hope somehow through the words God has given me, others will feel His peace.

I now realize that it was not my money or time that God wanted: it was my heart and my true faith and trust in Him. He wanted me to return to the faith I had as a child so many years ago. I must continue filling mailboxes with God's Word so that all can feel His peace in the world that surrounds them. I hope you will feel God's peace in all that surrounds you. I hope you will feel His peace in the words of this book.

I tell you the truth; anyone who will not receive the kingdom of God like a little child will never enter it. (Mark 10:1 NIV)

Thanksgiving

One of my favorite things to do is walk down the beach on a warm sunny day. I do it very seldom now, but when I do, it brings back many wonderful memories of my childhood and the hours we spent on the beach.

I was always barefoot; there was always a gentle breeze; and my mom and I, along with our friends, would walk, play, and collect shells for hours. We knew each shell by name, and when we found one we could not identify, we could not wait to go look it up in the shell book and see what it was. We would jump and play chase with the waves (never swimming because I was not allowed in past my knees), chase seagulls, build sandcastles, and bury our feet in the soft sand. We loved finding old pieces of driftwood, and a horse-shoe crab was a special treat. It was an endless adventure with treasures everywhere.

Today, when I walk down a beach, I relive those memories, and I am so thankful. I see not just treasures, but God's treasures. How awesome and beautiful He has made all things! He used these treasures, and still uses them today, to fill my heart with wonderful memories of time spent with those I love.

Look for the treasures in your life each day. Be thankful in all things and store the memories. Slow your life down enough so you can build precious memories with those you love. God's treasures are all around you, so enjoy them!

Every good and perfect gift comes from above. (James 1:17 NIV)

Dear Lord, I am thankful for everyone in my life and the memories we share. Thank You for the endless treasures that You have given us to enjoy, and thank You for sending Jesus who came to save us all and fill our hearts with love and joy. Amen.

Love, Grits

PS: We could have all the wealth in the world, but only when we come to know God's treasures will we be truly wealthy.

Up the Creek

I love the memories I have of growing up in the Low Country. One of my favorites is shrimping with my dad. We loved to shrimp and went often. He was a strong man, kind and humble, a man of few words—but I always knew his thoughts, and I just followed along.

One hot steamy day, we were up a small creek shrimping, and the catch was plentiful! We were so immersed in our success that we totally forgot to pay attention to the tide that was dropping fast. Before we knew it, we were stuck on the mudflat. I could tell by his expression—his furrowed brow and his pursed lips—that he was not very happy.

When our eyes met, we both burst out laughing. It was all we could do! As the old saying goes: "Up a creek without a paddle," that was us! We knew there was nothing we could do except wait for the tide to turn and come in. So we made the best of it, headed shrimp, laughed, and joked that Mom would probably send the Coast Guard out looking for us as it would be hours before we could get off the mudflat. Those were the days before cell phones! That memory of us is precious to me. Sitting there chipping the shrimpy ice block to quench our thirst—the two of us quietly, patiently waiting.

I often feel like I'm up a creek without a paddle. High and dry with nowhere to go. Life's challenges are just too much to handle. Nothing I can do to change the situation. I know I must turn to God again. I sometimes feel so guilty, as I am always asking Him for something. But I know, in my heart, He longs for me to reach out. I know He hears my prayers, and I know He will answer me. I may have to wait. His answer may not be exactly what I want, but I know it will be what is best for me. As I pray diligently, wait patiently, trust Him completely, I know the tide will turn.

> "For I know the plans I have for you," declares the LORD, "plans to prosper you and not to harm you, plans to give you hope and a future. Then you will call on me and come and pray to me, and I will listen to you. You will seek me and find me when you seek me with all your heart." (Jeremiah 29:11–19 NIV)

Dear Lord, thank You for precious memories. Thank You for always being there when I need You and never getting tired of my unending requests. Help me to be patient and accept the answers that You give me. Amen.

Love, Grits

PS: I asked God, "Why are You taking me through such troubled waters?" He replied, *Because your enemy can't swim.*

Fear

Sometimes I become so afraid. As strong as I feel my faith is, I have moments when I slip and wonder why or how or what will happen! I think it's just human nature to feel fearful at times.

The one positive thing about my fear is that it calls me back to my faith and reminds me of the strength God gives me to face each fear. It never ceases to amaze me when I read His word, pray, and give my fear over to God; He gives me back the peace that passes all understanding. I feel His presence, and I know He is by my side to help me conquer each fear one step at a time.

So give God your fears and let Him guide you. Let Him do all the worrying.

> Do not fear for I am with you; do not be dismayed for I am your God. I will strengthen you and help you; I will uphold you with my righteous right hand. (Isaiah 41:10 NIV)

Dear Lord, please take away our fear. You tell us not to fear, but we do. Forgive us when we are weak, and give us the strength to overcome our fears, knowing You have given us Your word that You will handle them. Thank You for always being there to remove our fear and replace it with Your perfect peace. Amen.

Love, Grits

PS: When fear knocks at your door, send faith out to meet him.

Patience

Fishing from a small boat in early spring is wonderful. The air is crisp and cool, but the warm sun quickly takes the chill away. Many days, my bait barely breaks the surface of the water before I get a bite. Other days, that cork bobs for hours before I get a bite, or I may not get one at all. I know the fish are there all around me, so close yet so far away. I have the right bait in the water, but they are just not ready to bite. Those days, I just bask in the warm sun, let the fresh air cleanse my mind, and patiently wait.

I often relate my fishing to God. Sometimes He answers my prayers immediately. Other times He makes me wait a long time. He may not answer my prayer at all, but I know He is there, surrounding me, just like the fish that I can't see. He knows every situation, and He knows what is best. I must sit and wait, feeling His warm love cleansing my soul while remaining confident of His presence.

When the time is right, He will answer my prayer or lead me in a new direction. I hope I will never stop fishing and casting my bait on those early spring days. I know I will never stop casting my prayers to God, knowing that He will always be there.

So be patient and confident. It makes for a good fisherman and a great Christian.

> Be strengthened with all power according to His glorious might so that you may
> have great endurance and patience. (Colossians 1:11 NIV)

Dear Lord, give me faith and confidence to face any situation that comes my way. Stay by my side and give me the patience to wait for Your perfect timing. Amen.

Love, Grits

PS: How can one match start a forest fire, but it takes a whole box to start a campfire?

The Gentle Breeze

I love sitting on my deck after a long hot summer day. The sun has gone down, a gentle breeze is blowing, and it is finally cooling down. I cannot see the breeze, but it is there. I see the leaves and the moss on the old oak tree flowing back and forth, and I feel the air gently brush against my skin.

God's spirit is a lot like the gentle breeze. We cannot see it, but it's there. It is working around us and in us. Like the breeze, we must learn to believe without seeing, to feel His presence and peace every day, and then to use His spirit within us to gently bring others to Him.

> The wind blows wherever it pleases. You hear its sound, but you cannot tell where it comes from or where it is going. (John 3:8 NIV)

> Jesus said to His disciples, "Because you have seen Me, you have believed; blessed are those who have not seen Me and yet believe." (John 20:29 NIV)

Dear Lord, I do not see the wind, but I know it is there. I do not see You, but I know You are there. Touch my heart that I may encourage others to feel Your presence through the whisper of the gentle breeze. Amen.

Love, Grits

PS: Never miss a rainbow or a sunset because you are always looking down.

China-Backs

When I heard the words "let's go catch China-backs," I knew my dad and I were off on another adventure. China-backs are the type of fiddler crabs we caught in the pluff mud at low tide to use as bait for sheepshead fishing. They are not like the drab brown fiddlers; instead their backs are brilliant in color and, for a fiddler, very beautiful.

Not only were the China-backs hard to catch, the sheepsheads were sometimes impossible! Covered in mud, hot and sweaty, carrying a bucket full of scurrying fiddlers, we headed to the old trestle on our mission to outwit the elusive sheepshead! And outwit us they usually did! Fiddler after fiddler, they sucked the bait off our hooks. No matter how hard we concentrated and tried to feel the slightest movement in the line to set the hook, they escaped us time after time. A bucket full of bait was empty in no time.

I learned a few choice words from my dad during our many fishing trips, but I learned really fast not to repeat them! The ratio of fish to fiddler was always very poor, but with a little luck, we usually managed to catch a few for my mom to bake for supper. I cherish the memories of those special times with my dad and only wish I could cook half as well as my mom.

Fishing taught me many things in life. It taught me that things in life don't always come easy. Being prepared, patient, and persistent, and never giving up are necessities for success. Trusting in something I may not be able to see, and feeling an ever so slight tug that I must not ignore, are all part of the lessons I will never forget.

Do you ever feel God pulling ever so slightly on your heart strings? Are you trying to feel His presence and follow His direction for your life? Is He asking you to be prepared, patient, and persistent? If so, set the hook and trust in His perfect timing: for being hooked on God is the greatest catch ever.

Dear Lord, please keep tugging at my heart. I might even need a good hard jerk every now and then to set the hook on this stubborn heart. I pray to be forever hooked on You. Amen.

Love, Grits

PS: And now they say mud is good for you. Put it all over your face and it works miracles! I should have a perfect complexion with all the mud I grew up in!

The Life Ring

Sometimes I feel like I am drowning in all the confusion, worries, and challenges of life. I try so hard to keep things under control, but I keep slipping farther into *chaos*.

As much as I would like to, I realize I can't do it alone. I need God to throw me a life ring. When I grab hold of His life ring, He pulls me gently to His safety and helps me through all the problems I am facing.

Pray for His help. Let God throw you His life ring. Reach out and grab hold. He can bring you in if you let Him, and together you can face all the challenges of your life.

God can save your life; let Him.

I have set before you life or death…choose life. (Deuteronomy 30:19 NIV)

Dear Lord, when we are in over our heads, thank You for being there to throw us Your life ring and pulling us gently to safety. Amen.

Love, Grits

PS: If you want to lift yourself up, lift someone else up.

Dear Lord, let us never stop loving each other as You have loved us. Help us to always take the time to spend with family and friends and always thank you for the many blessings we often overlook. Amen.

Love, Grits

PS: In making a living today, many no longer leave room for life.

Relationships

I really did not want to go. I was tired from work, had clothes to wash, and bills to pay, and then my husband asked me to go turkey hunting with him. It was the last day of the season; it was a beautiful afternoon, and I knew my chores could wait. A trip to the woods would refresh my mind and improve my attitude, and maybe I could get a picture of a big gobbler in strut. I said yes. I grabbed my camera, he grabbed his gun, and off we went.

The long road we walked to get to the perfect spot was filled with turkey- and deer tracks, always a good sign. We settled down shoulder to shoulder against a huge oak tree. It had been a long time since we had been hunting together. It felt good. I adjusted my camera, looked around, and realized I would never be able to get a picture today. Turkeys have excellent vision, and we were way too exposed for me to move at all.

Shortly after we settled in, he whispered, "I don't think that camera thing will work." I smiled to myself as I already knew that. I knew if I scared his turkey with my camera, it would be me he would carry back home by my feet, upside down over his shoulder, instead of a turkey!

It wasn't too long before the first two showed up: two hens leisurely strolling by. Our adrenaline started pumping, just knowing the big gobbler could be behind them. Time passed slowly. We waited patiently, but the big gobbler never showed. That did not matter to me as I was so content sitting next to my soul mate, enjoying time with him and the beautiful woods. I was so glad I had come. It had been a long time since the two of us were alone, silent, enjoying each other's company.

As the sun slowly set, we witnessed four or five turkeys fly into the trees close by where they would roost for the night. We quietly slipped out of the woods so we would not disturb them. No gobbler, but an awesome afternoon.

We slowly walked the long road back to the truck, serenaded by frogs, crickets, lightning bugs, and a few pesky mosquitoes. He finally spoke and said, "We put them to bed until next season." He seemed very content. I was so thankful I had come. That I had taken the time to stop and come to the woods. To enjoy God's beautiful creation and be with someone I love and so often take for granted. I hoped he was feeling the same. My soul was refreshed.

We must take time for relationships with our spouses, family, friends, and all those we love—especially God. Life is short and passes by quickly. The older I get, this old saying gets more real: "the days pass slowly, but the years fly by." We must take time to refresh our souls. God wants us to take time from our busy lives to share love with each other. To spend time with Him. Make the time. It's well worth the effort.

Be devoted to one another in brotherly love. Honor one another above yourselves.
(Romans 12:10 NIV)

Stuff Happens

Stuff happens! It just does.

Discouragement sets in and we feel hopeless. We have tried to take care of things on our own and failed. Then Satan comes in and tries to make his claim on our souls.

It is in the most discouraging, hopeless times that we must rely on our faith. We must believe that God loves us, is in control of our future, and knows what's best. God uses the stuff in our lives to strengthen us, to give us courage, and to show us what is really important. We have to let Him take control. Let Him fight our battles. Call on God for help while believing He will sort through our stuff and make a clear path for our lives.

> We know that in all things God works for the good of those who love Him, who have been called according to His purpose. (Romans 8:28 NIV)

> "For I know the plans I have for you," declares the Lord. "Plans to prosper you and not to harm you, plans to give you hope and a future." (Jeremiah 29:11 NIV)

Dear Lord, please be there to rescue us when stuff happens. We cannot do it alone. When chaos fills our lives, take over and give us Your peace, and show us the direction You have planned for us. Amen.

Love, Grits

PS: Miracles can't happen until you put your problems into God's hands.

Porch Swing

Crowded streets, crowded stores, crowded schedules, crowded lives—work, school, sports, and meetings. Busy, busy, busy. Long gone are the squeaky-porch-swing days, swinging for hours with loved ones and friends. Long gone are family devotions. There's barely enough time for a short prayer before bedtime. Long gone are family meals preceded by a blessing. Long gone are Sunday commitments to church and God. Our brains are on overload most of the time. Even phone calls to hear friendly familiar voices have been replaced by texts and emails.

I took the time recently to sit with my ninety-six-year-old neighbor, my "yard buddy," on his front porch. The pink azaleas he so tenderly cared for through the years were in full bloom, and the river beyond them continued its journey back to the ocean. We rocked and talked, and the things I needed to get home to do were no longer important. This special time with him was much more important than anything I needed to do.

I thought back to the times when he and I walked together in the yard, discussing flowers, trees, birds, and weeds. The valuable lessons he taught me will never be forgotten. As we sat and talked, I was amazed at his wisdom and knowledge. His memories of the past took me back to a time long ago. His adventures in the creek; stories of his work at the Navy Yard; and memories of Johns Island, when it truly was an undeveloped island, fascinated me. He painted a picture in my mind of a time when life was slower, work and loyalty were valued, and family and friendships were cherished. My time spent with him was priceless.

It's time to put the brakes on, slow down, and stop. We must start taking time for ourselves, our families, our friends, and God. God has given us so many blessings, and we are rushing by them every day without appreciating them. Life here on earth is very short. We must not wait to enjoy these blessings.

Jesus never missed a chance to comfort, talk, and help others. His life here on earth was so short, but what an impact He had on all who sat with Him and listened. He took the time to be a friend. He wants us to take time for others—to love and care for them. Can we stop long enough to visit with someone who could use a friend?

Make time to enjoy your family and friends. Make time to sit in the porch swing with Jesus.

Be still and know that I am God. (Psalm 46:10 NIV)

Dear Lord, help us to slow down and enjoy all that surrounds us. Help us spend time with family and friends, and to reach out to others who have no family. Thank You for all our blessings and especially for the love, joy, and peace that You give us each day. Amen.

Love, Grits

PS: Life is temporary. Love is forever.

The Anchor

The Coast Guard requires every boat to always have an anchor on board. If you break down, need to rest, or if you find a good fishing hole, the anchor allows you to stay safely in the same position while you get help, rest, or simply enjoy the moment.

I like to think of God as my spiritual anchor. If I am broken down, in need of a rest, or just enjoying life, He lets me throw out my anchor. He mends my troubles, gives me rest, and enjoys the pleasures of life along with me.

Let the Bible and God's presence be your anchor. Throw all your cares and concerns to Him in prayer. Anchor your soul in His mighty power. Then haul in your anchor and go on your way with renewed strength, hope, courage, and peace. You will be able to face whatever may come your way.

We have this hope as an anchor for the soul, firm and secure. (Hebrews 6:19 NIV)

Dear Lord, please be my anchor in all that I do. Let me take the time in this rushed world to stop and anchor my soul in Your word and prayer, then send me on my way to face each day with Your renewed strength and hope. Amen.

Love, Grits

PS: People don't care how much you know. They just need to know how much you care.

The Heart

The world has changed so much since the time when Jesus was born and lived. Modern inventions and technologies have made life so much easier and more comfortable. Electricity, automobiles, computers, television, and iPhones are just a few of the conveniences that make our lives easier.

Unfortunately, these great technologies and all the inventions of modern time cannot take away loneliness, fear, heartbreak and sadness. We will continue to face these problems in our hearts and souls every day. Medical advances can now repair many problems with our physical hearts, but only God can heal our broken spiritual hearts. Our only peace will come through our faith and hope in our Lord Jesus.

When Jesus lived among us, he went around comforting all those with heavy hearts. He forgave their sins, gave comfort to the lonely and heartbroken, and showed compassion wherever he went. He gave hope and strength and purpose to others just by showing love and concern.

Jesus is still here for us, showering us with His comfort, tenderness, compassion, forgiveness, and hope. All we need to do is invite Him into our hearts. Let Him heal the brokenness we feel. All He asks in return is for us to reach out and comfort, love, forgive, and support others.

Is there someone you can call, visit, send a card to, or pray for? It doesn't take a lot of money or time to show a little compassion and love for someone.

I think maybe one of the greatest gifts we could give to Jesus is to reach out and touch someone's heart and show them love and compassion. I'm sure it is what He would do.

> Praise be to the God and Father of our Lord Jesus Christ, the Father of compassion
> and the God of all comfort, who comforts us in all our troubles, so that we can comfort
> those in any trouble with the comfort we ourselves receive from God. (2 Corinthians 1:3
> NIV)

Dear Lord, please put compassion in our hearts and let us bring comfort, hope, and love to someone in need. Amen.

Love, Grits

PS: If you grasp tomorrow with faith, you know the handle won't fall off!

Treasures

As a child, I always dreamed of finding a pirate's treasure chest hidden in my yard or underneath the sand at the beach. How exciting it would have been to dig it up, open it, and find it overflowing with gold, silver, and jewels! Of course I never found one, but how fun it was to imagine.

I now have found a much greater treasure: my Bible. I find treasures every time I open it. It may be an underlined verse from the past or a new verse I missed the first time around. I love to read stories about the heroes of the past, their great faith and trust, and the miracles God did for them. I think about them so often as I see the miracles He performs in my life. These stories give me wisdom, courage, and strength to face each day.

The Bible gives me instructions on how to live a good, honest, caring, giving life. It teaches me to pray and to trust. It teaches me to forgive and to love. It gives me peace. These treasures are far more valuable than silver, gold, and jewels could ever be.

Open your treasure chest, and you will be amazed.

> I will give you hidden treasures; riches stored in secret places; so that you may know that I am the Lord. (Isaiah 45:3 NIV)

> In whom are hidden all the treasures of wisdom and knowledge. (Colossians 2:3 NIV)

Dear Lord, help me to be ever reminded of all the valuable treasures awaiting me every time I read Your Word. Help me to take the time to search for these treasures deep within the depths of its pages. Keep the memory of these treasures in my heart, assuring me that You are truly my Lord and Savior. Amen.

Love, Grits

PS: The heart is like a treasure chest that's filled with souvenirs: it's where we keep the memories we've gathered through the years.

The Compass

Have you ever experienced being lost in the woods? That feeling of panic and fear when you realize you are deep in the woods with no idea how to get out? It's not a good feeling! Every tree looks alike; every path seems the same; the sun is blocked by the treetops; and the more you walk, the more you realize you are completely lost. Panic is about to overcome you when you suddenly remember that your iPhone has a compass app. What a relief it is when you realize it can lead you safely out of the woods.

Life can often feel like being lost in a great big forest, surrounded by so many possibilities and decisions to make, so many paths to choose from, and no clear direction to go. Frightened and overwhelmed, we realize it's time to turn to our spiritual compass. God is willing and able to help us with all of these decisions. He waits patiently for us to ask for His guidance. So pull out your spiritual compass and let God help you through this confusing forest of life.

> I will instruct you and teach you in the way you should go: I will counsel you with my eye upon you. (Psalm 32:8 NIV)

> Show me Your ways, oh Lord, teach me Your paths. Guide me in Your truth and teach me. (Psalm 25:4–5 NIV)

Dear Lord, when we become so lost and confused with the decisions we must make each day, let us remember to take the time to ask for Your guidance. Be our compass. Make our paths clear, and be our spiritual compass through this vast wilderness of life. Amen.

Love, Grits

PS: If God is your co-pilot, swap seats.

Tough Times

I am learning to appreciate tough times. Certainly I don't like them, but I love knowing I can call out to the Lord and ask Him to carry my burdens. When I truly turn my burdens over to Him, my hardships turn into opportunities—wonderful opportunities to be closer to God, relying on His strength, feeling His peace, and trusting in His plan.

Don't wait until you are weary and tired to finally call out for help. Give Him your burdens each day in everything you face. The road ahead will be much easier to travel knowing He will do what is best for your life.

But the salvation of the righteous is from the Lord. He is their strength in times of trouble. The Lord shall help them and deliver them. He shall deliver them from the wicked and save them, because they trust in Him. (Psalm 37:39–40 KJV)

Dear Lord, You told us when You were here on earth, "Come to Me, all you that are weary and are heavy-laden, and I will give you rest. Take My yoke upon you, and learn from Me; for I am gentle and humble in heart, and you will find rest for your souls" (Matthew 11:28 KJV).

We ask You, Lord, "Come, Lord Jesus, come." Amen.

Love, Grits

PS: God may not do what you want, but He will do what is right and best.

The Cross

It was a long day. It was a difficult day. Work had been stressful for months, and the reality of going into the slow winter months was frightening. My daughter was waiting on biopsy results for cancer, and a dear friend had just overdosed on drugs. My heart was heavy. I prayed so hard and tried to stay strong, but I felt so empty inside.

The river was calling me when I got home from work. I had so much to do, but I needed to escape reality for a while, and the river is always my peace. It was a beautiful high tide. I got in my kayak and paddled and prayed, hoping for peace and answers.

As I entered a small cove near sunset, I looked up and saw the figure of a cross. At first I thought someone had put a cross in the marsh, but I quickly realized it was two branches making the perfect cross. If I moved to the right or left, it disappeared, so I positioned myself right in front of it. It was amazing.

As the sun slowly set behind it, I was moved to tears of thankfulness for this beautiful moment in time. I felt God's presence so close and real. I knew He was telling me to leave my worries, troubles, and fears at the foot of this cross, and let Him carry the burdens I was carrying. And so I did. As the tears and prayers flowed, I released it all to Him. Slowly I felt the peace I was searching for. My soul was refreshed.

Daylight was fading, and I knew I had to go home. I wanted so badly to stay and continue feeling the peace, comfort, and love that God had just shared with me. It was all I could do to paddle away. I knew God had clearly spoken to me. He held me and reassured me that He was with me and that He would never leave me. I was at peace. I could face the road ahead.

As I headed toward home, a beautiful hymn—"When Peace Like a River" by Horatio G. Spafford— came to mind, and I sang it over and over all the way home.

"When peace like a river, attendeth my way; when sorrows like sea billows roll,
Whatever my lot, God has taught me to say, 'it is well, it is well with my soul.'"

People often ask me how I hear God speak. The only answer I know is to look and listen for that quiet voice. It may be anywhere. He won't shout or yell; it will be the quiet voice speaking to you through the quiet and beauty of the simplest everyday things around you. But you must take time to listen. And you will know when He does. You will just know.

Whether you turn to the right or to the left, your ears will hear a voice behind you,
saying, "This is the way; walk in it." (Isaiah 30:21 NIV)

Love, Grits

PS: Remember that you may be the lighthouse in someone else's storm.

Sit at the Feet of Jesus

Mary sat at the feet of Jesus soaking in all that He said and taught. Martha continued to prepare the meal alone, her anger growing because Mary was not helping her. When Martha finally had enough, she confronted Jesus. "Lord, don't you care that my sister has left me to do all the work myself? Tell her to help me!"

Jesus replied, "You are worried and upset about many things, but only one thing is needed. Mary has chosen what is better, and it will not be taken from her."

How often do we feel overwhelmed and alone doing all the work? No one else seems to be helping at all. How often do we stay so busy with our daily chores and events that we neglect to sit with Jesus, read His Word, and listen to His voice? How often do we miss the chance to feel His guidance and peace each day?

What better decisions we would make, what comfort and peace we would feel if we would just stop and make time for Jesus. He longs for our time. Each day He longs to give us strength to face each trial and fear. He wants us to be like Mary, taking time in this busy-and-hectic world to sit by His side listening to all He has to tell us.

> "Lord, don't you care that my sister has left me to do the work by myself? Tell her to help me!" "Martha, Martha," the Lord answered. "You are worried and upset about many things, but only one thing is needed. Mary has chosen what is better, and it will not be taken away from her." (Luke 10:40–41 NIV)

Dear Lord, help us be more like Mary, taking time to sit at Your feet, listening to Your stories, and feeling Your peace. Help us choose You over the world. In this fast and whirlwind world, we desperately need this time to be with You. Amen.

Love, Grits

PS: Knowledge speaks, but wisdom listens.

Love

We hear and see the word everywhere. How do we recognize real love? What is real love? How do we know when love fills our hearts? Is love a deep friendship, sharing our hopes and dreams, successes and failures? Is love affection for others, making us feel good and secure? Is love passion, fulfilling all of our wants, desires, and needs? Is this love all about us and how it makes us feel? Is this real love?

If we look at the life of Jesus, we can learn something about real love. Jesus put everyone else's needs before his own. He never wanted anything for himself. He loved the unlovable, He had compassion for the sick, and He gave His time to teach the love of God to all. He suffered and gave His life to save all. His love for everyone was beyond anything we could ever imagine.

So if we follow the life and teachings of Jesus, we learn that love should be about how we make others feel and what we can do for them. Desiring what is best for those we care for. Making them better people through encouragement and support. Standing by them when they stumble and fall. Enjoying their joy and laughter, sadness and tears. Putting others' needs ahead of our own. Loving the unlovable. It is then that we are able to find real love. Stop seeking what love can do for us, and seek what we can do for love. And there we may find the love we have been searching for.

> "'Love the Lord your God with all your heart, with all your soul and with all your mind.' This is the first and greatest commandment. And the second is: 'Love thy neighbor as thyself.'" (Matthew 22:37–39 NIV)

Dear Lord, help us to know and find real love. Help us to put others' needs before our own, for only then will we find real love. Give us patience and kindness when we need it most. Help us to think of others before ourselves, just as You do for us every single day. We thank You for loving us enough to give Your life for us. Amen.

Love, Grits

PS: If there is anything better than being loved, it is loving.

The Tide

I sat on the dock watching as the tide eased in, letting all the stresses of the day fade away. The osprey, claws gripping tightly to a freshly caught fish, brought food to his nest. The egrets slowly strolled the bank in search of supper. At the river's edge, the fish feasted on schools of minnows and shrimp. The great blue heron stood tall in the marsh grass, and the seagulls flew gracefully overhead. The tide stopped, and time stood still. For only a second. As if to say, "rest, find peace in the stillness, for there is more work ahead."

Our lives are so full and stressful. We need to be like the tides. Stop, rest, and regroup—if only for a short time. Let God bring you peace so when the tide turns, you will be ready to face whatever is before you.

> But ask the animals, and they will teach you, or the birds in the sky, and they will tell you; or speak to the earth, and it will teach you, or let the fish in the sea inform you. Which of all these does not know that the hand of the Lord has done this? In his hand is the life of every creature and the breath of all mankind. (Job 12:7–10 NIV)

> And on the seventh day God rested. (Genesis 2:2 NIV)

Dear Lord, thank You for the beauty around us. Help us to feel Your peace and learn from this awesome beauty. Teach us to rest. May we always be thankful for creation, but may we never forget the awesome Creator. Amen.

Love, Grits

PS: There is no greater proof of God than in the beauty of nature.

Starfish

Starfish is a swimming term used when teaching young children how to save themselves from drowning. They are taught to roll onto their backs and float like a starfish until someone can help them. It is an amazing life-saving technique that has saved so many children. We witnessed it firsthand when we saw how it saved our niece, and I would recommend it to every parent who has their infant or small child near a pool, lake, river, or any water! It is also an excellent technique for adults to know.

I was caught in a rip tide at the beach one day, scared and close to panic. Finally I quit fighting the current, rolled onto my back, and waited until I had drifted out of the danger. Little did I know I had "star-fished," but looking back, it is exactly what I did, and it probably saved my life.

So many days I feel like I am in way over my head and can barely keep my head above water. The harder I swim, the farther away from shore I get! I finally realize I cannot do it alone. I need to roll on my back and "starfish" for a while.

I need to call on the Lord and ask Him to rescue me from my troubling waters. I know He is the only one that can help me. I must trust that He will rescue me and bring me safely to shore. I need to ask Him to stay by my side, rescue me from the troubling waters, and guide me through every circumstance and decision I face each day.

> Now on one of those days Jesus and His disciples got into a boat, and He said to them, "Let us go over to the other side of the lake." So they launched out. But as they were sailing along, He fell asleep; and a fierce gale of wind descended on the lake, and they began to be swamped and to be in danger. They came to Jesus and woke Him up, saying, "Master, Master, we are drowning!" And He got up and rebuked the wind and the surging waves, and they stopped, and it became calm. (Luke 8:22–24 NIV)

Dear Lord, thank You for always being my lifeguard. Help me always remember to "starfish" and wait for You to rescue me. Amen.

Love, Grits

PS: Be strong enough to stand alone, smart enough to know when you need help, and brave enough to ask for it.

To find swimming lessons in your area, visit their website, ISR Infant Swimming Resource. Their motto is: "Not one more child drowns."

Emptiness

I claim to have such great faith and trust. In times of trouble, I claim that my faith and trust remove my fear. So what is this emptiness that overcomes me in the midst of my trials? I try so hard to stay strong, but so often I fail. I feel so guilty continually calling on God to strengthen me and drive out this fear, pleading for answers, strength, and peace, and praying so hard for patience as I wait for answers. Where is that great faith and trust I proclaim to have?

I may not understand my weakness, but God does. He knows when I am weak, and He knows when I am strong. I know He longs for me to come back to Him in prayer over and over again. I am assured that He forgives my weakness and fills me again with His reassurance of love and peace. He knows my faith and trust are strong, but only with the support of His constant presence. We will never be strong enough to conquer fear on our own. I will continue to call upon God. I will continue to read His Word. I will trust Him to strengthen my faith. In each weak moment, He awaits my call. I just need to trust Him.

In my weakness, I seek Him more. In my prayer, He forgives me more.

Through my faith, He calms my fears, gives me strength, and wipes each tear. (Unknown)

May the God of hope fill you with all joy and peace as you trust in Him, so that you may overflow with hope by the power of the Holy Spirit. (Romans 15:13 NIV)

Dear Lord, please forgive me when I feel empty. My faith is strong, and I trust You. I just need Your constant presence to fill that empty feeling, to reassure my faith and trust as I wait patiently for Your answers. Amen.

Love, Grits

PS: When you get to the end of your rope, tie a knot, hang on, and pray.

Saltwater Veins

I am totally convinced that I have saltwater flowing through my veins—a definite inheritance from my father and my grandfathers, who all loved the water and fishing. My most vivid memories are of the life I spent on the rivers, creeks, and oceans of the Low Country. And, to this day, I can never get enough of all it has to offer.

The education I received from my father is priceless. He not only taught me everything I know, but the experiences we shared together are irreplaceable to me. I long for those days shrimping, boating, fishing, crabbing, gigging, and just loving the salt life with him, sharing God's great creation. I would not trade these memories for anything in this world.

Since then, I have taught my children, and now my grandchildren, what I learned through the years. I see the excitement as they catch a crab, throw the net for shrimp, and catch fish and stingrays from the dock. I see the excitement in their eyes and their spirit of adventure when they paddle across the creek to the mudflat and then return covered from head to toe in pluff mud, belly laughing as they look at one another!

Time spent with them is precious and passing. I thank God for the saltwater in my veins and the blessing of being able to pass on the beauty and joy of His creation to the next generation. I just hope their veins will flow with saltwater. I can think of nothing better to pass on to them—other than my faith.

What passion runs through your veins? Your love of the sand, mountains, wildlife, art? The list goes on and on. Take what you love and pass it on to friends and loved ones. Share it with them and build precious memories. Teach them to see God's presence in the midst of your passion, whatever it may be, so that maybe one day their veins will flow with the passion you shared.

> We will not hide them from their children, but tell to the coming generation the glorious deeds of the LORD, and his might, and the wonders that he has done. (Psalm 78:4 ESV)

> Let the heavens rejoice, let the earth be glad; let the sea resound, and all that is in it. Let the fields be jubilant, and everything in them; let all the trees of the forest sing for joy. (Psalm 96:11–12 NIV)

Dear Lord, thank You for all of the beauty around us. Help us to always see Your hand in all of creation, and help us to pass this on from generation to generation. Amen.

Love, Grits

PS: When prayer becomes your habit, miracles become your lifestyle.

My Osprey

Last spring, I was fortunate enough to be able to observe two ospreys build their nest on a platform in the marsh across from my house. How fascinating to watch the way they worked together. The mom and dad were busily coming and going until they were satisfied that the nest was complete, and then the mom sat on the egg while the dad brought fresh fish for their meals. Sometimes he would give her a break and sit on the egg himself until she returned. It was almost like the changing of the guards.

Day in and day out, they continued until the day the egg finally hatched. And even then they continued their vigil with one standing guard over the nest while the other brought food home. I was thrilled the first time I saw that tiny head look over the edge of the nest.

Day after day, I watched as they fed the baby beak-to-beak. I watched as the baby finally learned to sit on the edge of the nest while the mom was teaching it to be watchful and alert. I watched as the mom held it back when it tried to leave the nest too early. I was so looking forward to the day when the young osprey would spread its wings and fly. It was only days away from leaving the nest when tragedy struck. The nest was hit by lightning and caught fire. The parents escaped, but the baby did not survive.

The osprey parents screamed and flew around the destroyed nest for days as they mourned the loss of their baby. I was devastated. How could this have happened to this precious baby bird? I cried and asked God, "Why? Oh why?" I had no answer.

I thought of the recent death of a friend's child and could not even imagine the hurt and pain they must be feeling! I prayed for their peace. I had a vision of that precious child running in heaven with my baby osprey flying close behind, then landing on his shoulder when he stopped. Two best buddies. I still don't understand. I never will.

I just know that as I prayed and pictured these two beautiful angels in heaven, I realized God did have a reason, and we must accept that He has a bigger and better plan beyond our understanding. We have to believe and trust in Him and look forward to the day we will be reunited with all the beautiful angels He called before us. We will never understand death, nor are we supposed to. What God has called us to do is to trust Him and feel the peace only He can give us.

Dear Lord, I know, without a doubt, that these two babies are frolicking together in heaven. Please give peace to all families who have lost loved ones, some way too soon. Give them the peace only You can provide and the hope and reassurance that they will be together again. In Your name we pray, amen.

Love, Grits

PS: We often look so long at the closed door that we do not see the one which opens for us.

The Letters

Sometimes in life we don't know what we have until it is gone. Looking back, I realize the love between my parents was a treasure I never appreciated or completely understood until they were gone. I remember the loving way they looked at each other; the care and concern and affection they showed. The loving smiles they shared when their eyes met, holding hands wherever they went, or a simple hug for no reason. These are just a few of the beautiful things they shared. They were there for each other through good times and through hard times.

As they grew older, I saw a love that could never be taken away, not even through death. They were a part of a great generation that valued friendship, commitment, and love. Their faith was strong, their loyalty true. They were *the greatest generation.*

I was fortunate enough to find hundreds of love letters my parents exchanged during World War II. One was dated December 6, 1941, mailed the day before Pearl Harbor was bombed. This letter describes a normal day in the life of a sailor with no indication of any upcoming danger.

The next day, the world changed forever. These awesome letters paint a vivid picture of love and war. Each letter portrays their faith in God, commitment to our country, and love for each other and family. They were a generation with respect for all and appreciation for the little they had. They sacrificed so much for us. They would have given their lives for our freedom.

They waited weeks for letters from each other as there was no telephone communication, and it took over a week to travel by train across the country. They made me realize how rare these values are today, and how totally spoiled this generation is. I have come to appreciate so much more the hardships they endured for freedom and love. I wish I was a film producer and could make a movie from their letters as it would be the most beautiful love story that could be told.

It made me realize how much our servicemen and their families sacrifice to keep this nation safe and how true love prevails. If I could write my life story in letters, what would they tell to others?

> Love is patient, love is kind. It does not envy, it does not boast, it is not proud. It is not rude, it is not self-seeking, it is not easily angered, it keeps no record of wrongs. Love does not delight in evil but rejoices with the truth. It always protects, always trusts, always hopes, always perseveres. Love never fails… (1 Corinthians 13:4–8 NIV)

Thank You, Lord, for these treasured letters. I pray they will make me a better person. I pray I will love deeper, respect others, and be thankful for all I have. Help me to always be a role model for my children, and hopefully one day they will appreciate it. Thank You for these precious letters that paint such a beautiful story of love and faith through some of the hardest times in their lives. Amen.

Love, Grits

PS: I love you.

Exercising

To become strong, we must continually exercise and strengthen our muscles. If we don't, these muscles become small and weak. It is so hard to stay committed to a strengthening routine day after day. It's so easy to put it off until another day. But we know the results when we remain faithful to workouts, so we must push ourselves to be committed each day.

Faith is like our muscles. We must exercise it continually. Through ups and downs, we must continue to work on our faith. We must keep it strong so that in the midst of unknown and trying times, our faith will give us strength to go on. The more we learn, read, pray, care, love, and understand God's Word, the more our faith is strengthened, and our trust in God will grow.

Keep exercising physically and spiritually. The results are well worth the efforts.

Dear Lord, help us to be committed to strengthening our bodies and our faith. Help us to be able to endure all that we face in this life through the faith and trust we build in You. Amen.

Love, Grits

PS: The expert in anything was once a beginner.

Foundations

Birds never cease to amaze me. I have watched so many build their strong intricate nests. The mom and dad continually bring twigs and leaves until they are satisfied that it is strong, safe, and secure. I have watched the male bird feed the female as she sits on eggs, and I have seen both guard the nest and then feed the young after they are hatched. I have seen ferocious storms—even hurricanes—come, but the little birds remain safe and protected from the storm.

God provides this security and protection for us if we build a strong foundation based on faith. The lightning may come, the thunder may roar, the waves may slam against the shore, but we need not worry if our foundation is strong. He will be in the midst of every storm in our lives and bring us peace and comfort. As the birds build their nests twig by twig, let us build our faith, scripture by scripture, prayer by prayer.

> I will put you in the cleft of the rock and will cover you with My hand until I have passed. (Exodus 33:22 NIV)

> The Lord is my rock, my fortress, and my deliverer. The Lord is my rock in whom I take refuge. (Psalm 18:2 NIV)

That is God's promise to us. We are secure in His hands forever. The storm rages, but our hearts are at rest.

Dear Lord, protect us from all the storms in our lives. Let us continually build our faith through scripture and prayer. Help us to never doubt You and have complete faith and trust You will be there to protect us. Amen.

Love, Grits

PS: Worry is like sitting in a rocking chair. It will give you something to do but will get you nowhere.

The Sunset

I was tired when I arrived home from work. I just wanted to sit and do nothing. I looked toward the river, and the high tide seemed to beckon me to go on a kayak ride. So I did. The sky was dreary and gray, and there seemed to be no wildlife stirring. I paddled farther up the creek and just let the troubles of the day drift off with the tide and enjoyed the peace the creek and marshlands always give me.

Then when I turned to go home, that gray dreary cloudy sky had turned into one of the most awesome sunsets I have ever seen. The sun itself was reflecting in the water, and the colors of the sky were indescribable. All I could do was stop and thank God for such a wonderful, joyous, refreshing sight.

As the sun slowly disappeared behind the marsh grass, I began to realize how God can take the ordinary, gray, cloudy times of our lives and transform them into times of extraordinary hope. Hope for our lives, our dreams, and our futures.

God spoke to me that day through the beauty of that unexpected glorious sunset. I felt His presence, and He refreshed my soul. We need to look for the simple beauty around us, feel God's presence, and let Him refresh and restore our souls.

> The Lord is my shepherd, I shall not want. He maketh me to lie down in green pastures: He leadeth me beside the still waters, He restoreth my soul. He leadeth me in the paths of righteousness for his name's sake. Yea, though I walk through the valley of the shadow of death, I will fear no evil: for Thou art with me; Thy rod and Thy staff they comfort me. Thou preparest a table before me in the presence of my enemies: Thou anointest my head with oil, my cup runneth over. Surely goodness and mercy shall follow me all the days of my life, and I will dwell in the house of the Lord forever. (Psalm 23 KJV)

Dear Lord, please help us to know that You are always with us and You can take all the troubles of this life and transform them into the hope and dreams for our future. Keep us safe, give us peace, protect us from danger, and anoint us with Your Holy Spirit so that we truly will dwell in Your house forever. Amen.

Love, Grits

PS: Life isn't about finding yourself; life is about creating yourself.

Reaching the Top

I am not a mountain climber, so I can only imagine how one must feel halfway up a steep mountain—too far up to go back, but a long steep rugged path ahead to the top. I can only compare it to my experience climbing to the top of a lighthouse.

Legs burning, hot and sweaty, ready to go back down but determined to make it to the top, I continued. I know that climbing a lighthouse does not even compare to climbing a mountain, and I would never attempt to be a mountain climber. I'm sure they have to constantly rest, regroup, and concentrate on where they are and where they need to be. I'm sure they have trained countless hours to prepare physically and mentally for the path ahead and then, with courage and strength, one step at a time, they finally reach their destination.

The awesome beauty they behold at the top makes it all worthwhile. My destination at the top of the lighthouse was breathtaking, so I can imagine a little of their satisfaction and joy.

Life for us, sometimes, is a steep rugged climb. The past is gone, and the uncertain future lies ahead. Like the mountain climber, we need to rest a while along the way. We need to focus our attention on God, asking for His guidance, reading His instructions, and asking Him to give us the strength to then move forward one step at a time, trusting that He will fully equip us with all we need to prepare us for whatever awaits us on the journey ahead. I can only imagine that the final destination will be breathtaking.

I am with you and will watch over you wherever you go. (Genesis 28:15 NIV)

Dear Lord, please help us learn how to rest with You. Please be our Companion and our Trainer. Give us strength and courage to face each day. Don't let our feet slip. Take our hand and guide us safely up all the steep mountains of this life. Amen.

Love, Grits

PS: Only those who will risk going too far can possibly find out how far one can go.

Guilt

Have you ever done something you just were not proud of? You said or did something that hurt a friend, a family member, yourself, or even a perfect stranger? You are miserable because you not only let yourself and everyone around you down, you know you let God down.

But God has a way to take us and our hurtful pasts and use it for His good. It begins with a simple prayer from you asking for forgiveness and help. He then will take all the broken pieces of your life, put them back together, and create a new you. He will give you the courage, strength, joy, and love you need to do great things with your life. God will forgive you.

The hardest part will be forgiving yourself, but with God's help, you can. Release the guilt within yourself and begin living the life God intends you to live.

> For God did not send His Son into the world to condemn the world, but that the world through Him might be saved. (John 3:17 NIV)

> This is a true saying, to be completely accepted and believed: Christ Jesus came into the world to save sinners. I am the worst of them. (1 Timothy 1:15 GNT)

Dear Lord, please forgive us if we have hurt anyone. Help us to forgive others and ourselves as You always forgive us. Use our mistakes to make us the servants You want us to be. Amen.

Love, Grits

PS: Bitterness and anger come back to hurt you much more than they hurt anyone else. Let it go.

Holy Week

Holy Week, which includes Easter Sunday and the six days leading up to it, is the most important week of a Christian's life. It is the week that God assures us we don't have to live in misery, sorrow, or regret of sin, but instead we will have everlasting life.

It is the week Jesus suffered His greatest hurt and pain. He entered Jerusalem to people shouting, "Hosanna to the King," but the week ended up very differently. People hurt Him. Friends denied Him. Officials hated Him. They crucified Him and nailed Him to the cross.

As He hung there, blood seeping through the nail holes in His body, He could have said, "I hate you, I will never forgive you, I hope you rot in hell." But instead, as He died for us, He said the most fascinating words, "Father, forgive them."

Three days later He arose.

How awesome to know that, as believers, our sins are forgiven. All we have to do is ask. What peace we have knowing that, as Christians, we have the hope of everlasting life. All we have to do is believe. As Christians, let us always remember to shout, "Hosanna to the King."

Are there people in our lives we need to forgive today? Are there others we need to share our hope with?

For God so loved the world that He gave His only begotten son, that whoever believes in Him will not perish but have everlasting life. (John 3:16 NIV)

Dear Lord, thank You for giving Your life so that we may have everlasting life. Your pain and suffering we can never fathom, but the love we feel is everlasting and real. Help us to forgive others as You forgive us, and thank You for the gift of everlasting life. Amen.

Love, Grits

PS: It is always the time to do what is right.

A Father's Smile

That smile. I will never forget that smile.

As I looked up from the cockpit to the bridge of the boat, I saw my father's beautiful smile. We had just landed what we thought could be the winning blue marlin in the Bohicket Marina Billfish Tournament. I was exhausted, knowing that only adrenaline had gotten me through the hour-and-forty minute fight.

The day only got better as my dad, who was the captain, was able to locate more fish, and all three of his children caught billfish that day! Not an easy feat in South Carolina in the early 1980s. Each time we caught a fish and I looked up at my dad, that smile got bigger and brighter. That smile will forever be etched in my mind. What a joyful blessed day.

I often look up to the heavens and hope that my Heavenly Father is looking down and smiling on me. I try hard to please Him. I fail so often, but I do try. When I become weak, I feel His adrenaline flowing through me, inspiring me to continue the good-and-challenging fight. I hope my love, kindness, and encouraging words will lead others into the arms of Almighty God. I will continue to look up and fight for that beautiful smile.

"Come, follow me," Jesus said, "and I will make you fishers of men." (Matthew 4:19 NIV)

So go out into the world and become fishers of men.

Love, Grits

PS: We did win the tournament with a 525 lb. blue marlin. It was a women's state record for twenty-five years. What an awesome memory.

PPS: Your miracles, along with your scars, are your testimony. Tell your story.

Feelings

Do you ever find it difficult to understand your feelings? You are hurt, disappointed, or depressed, and your dreams are slipping away. Nothing you say or do makes any difference. You want to solve all your problems yourself, but the more you try the worse it gets. You can't do it alone. Where do you turn?

You turn to Jesus. He is the Healer, the Provider, and the One who can make your dreams come true. He can mend your broken heart and guide you to your dreams. Jesus was born to experience what you are feeling and to understand your inner struggles. During His time on earth, He also felt hurt, disappointment, fear, sadness, and rejection. He feels our hurt, disappointment, fear, sadness, and rejection. He knows every tear we cry and hears every prayer we lift up to Him. He understands because He felt it all. He knows exactly how to restore your heart and comfort your soul.

Ask Jesus for help. He knows. He understands. Fall to your knees and ask Him into your heart, and then trust Him.

> He kept me safe when my city was under attack. In panic I cried out. But you heard my cry for mercy and answered my call for help. (Psalms 31:21–22 NLT)

Dear Lord, come into our hearts and heal our weary souls. Thank You that You understand the hurdles we face and are willing to be by our side all the way. Amen.

Love, Grits

PS: Every time you meet with God, it affects you in a positive way.

Choices

Being a Christian means that one part of you is constantly wanting to do right while the other part is desperately calling you into sin.

Fall to your knees. Fight these struggling forces through prayer and worship. As you let God into your life, He will sustain you through the perilous times of inner struggle. He will direct your paths, and together you will be able to make the right choices. You will continue to sin; we all will, but through prayer and worship, we can become the person God is calling us to be.

For we all have sinned and fall short of the glory of God. (Romans 3:23 NIV)

And He arose, and rebuked the wind, and said unto the sea, "Peace, be still." And the wind ceased and there was a great calm. (Mark 4:39 KJV)

Dear Lord, we all struggle. We are all sinners. We try hard but fail. Help us continue to turn to You for forgiveness, and help us each day to make the choices You want us to make.

Amen.

Love, Grits

PS: Linda Beery, a faithful friend who has now gone to live in heaven, sent this quote, and it is such a true statement: "All saints have a past, and all sinners have a future."

My Christmas Miracle

It was Christmas, my favorite time of the year. The tree was up, the presents wrapped, the house decorated. The craziness and rush were over. But something was missing. I felt guilty and empty. I had spent so much time and money on making everything perfect that I had lost the real meaning of Christmas.

I listened to Christmas carols, I did my devotions, I sent out my Christmas cards, but what had I really done for someone in need? Nothing. I was so ashamed as I entered church that Sunday. I just prayed, "Please, Lord, help me find someone in need. Forgive me for thinking only of myself and my loved ones and not thinking about the poor, lonely, homeless, or depressed. Please, Lord, help me."

As I drove up my driveway, the phone rang. It was a friend who asked if I could help with some food for someone she had happened to run into. He had lost his job and been evicted from his house, was hungry and really struggling, ready to give up. I looked to the sky and knew this was an answer to my prayer. I told her I would pay for a hotel room for him for the night, and maybe she could give him some food.

I quickly called and booked a room. She left to find him and tell him where to go. The more I thought about it, I knew I could not let him check out on Christmas Day! So I called and booked another day. I could at least do that. I prayed so hard for him.

The day after Christmas, my friend called, elated. The homeless man had found a job at a local camp-site, and it included a small trailer for him to live in. He was so thankful for the room and food and for the hope that our kindness had given him to continue on. God answered our prayers. I witnessed a true Christmas miracle. My emptiness was gone. I was filled with love, hope, and compassion.

We never know when the simplest act of kindness may change a person's life! We never know when God will use us for His purposes. God works His miracles through us with simple acts of kindness and love. We must be His hands and feet here on earth and listen when He calls!

That Christmas, God changed my life through a complete stranger. I saw how one simple act could change a person's life. I have no idea whatever happened to this stranger, but I continue to pray for him, and I know he is in God's hands. I did the part God led me to do, and He took over from there. I now make it a point to try to do something for someone in need every Christmas. I pray He will take my smallest act of kindness and turn it into someone's Christmas miracle!

He performs wonders that cannot be fathomed, miracles that cannot be counted. (Job 9:10 NIV)

Dear Lord, fill my heart with compassion. Use me and lead me wherever I can be of help to others. Help me to show love and kindness to all. And thank You for my special Christmas miracle. Amen.

Love, Grits

PS: You must be the change you wish to see in the world.

Exhausted

No matter how we add it up, we see no way our resources will stretch any more to cover our needs. We've done all we can and are exhausted. We have run out of options and have nowhere to turn.

It feels kind of like having an empty canteen in the desert. We have done everything we can possibly do on our own. At this point, there is only one way out: throw yourself at the mercy of God.

Now He can do His work. His resources never fail. Trust Him.

With God we gain victory, and He will trample down our enemies. (Psalm 60:12 NIV)

Dear Lord, I praise You for Your mercy. It is so hard to turn loose because we always want to be in control. But I know Your power only comes when we completely surrender our problems to You. I don't know how You will help us, but I'm thankful that You will. Thank You for being in control. Amen.

Love, Grits

PS: God does not call the equipped; He equips the called.

PPS: "God won't part the water in front of you until you take your first steps of faith." (Pastor Rick)

COVID-19

Why, God? A pandemic no one saw coming: COVID-19, February 2020. Everyone in fear for their lives and the lives of their loved ones. Businesses, schools, parks, restaurants, waterways, and even churches all closed worldwide. The economies of the world crashing. No end in sight.

Isolated in our homes, confused, frustrated, and scared, we call out to God. Help us. God tells us He works all trials for the best for us, but this makes no sense. Were we becoming overconfident, self-centered, and too comfortable in our daily lives? Were we overlooking those in need? Were we forgetting to thank God for all our blessings? Were we forgetting to pray and worship? Maybe we were taking our families for granted.

Whatever the case, God wants us to regroup and reconsider our priorities. He wants these hardships to remind us to call upon Him for help to give us wisdom and peace. He wants us to slow down and get to know Him better, trusting Him and believing He will see us through this. He wants us to learn to read His Word and expect an answer for our prayers.

I am sure He wants us to be better people, stronger Christians, full of love and godly wisdom. He wants a revival and *we* have to *be* the revival. There is a reason; there will be healing. It may not be immediate, but be confident He will take care of His children.

When I shut up the heavens so that there is no rain, or command locusts to devour the land or send a plague among my people, if my people, who are called by my name, will humble themselves and pray and seek my face and turn from their wicked ways, then will I hear from heaven and will forgive their sin and will heal their land. (2 Chronicles 7:13–14 NIV)

Cast your cares on the Lord and He will sustain you; He will never let the righteous fail. (Psalm 55:22 NIV)

Dear Lord, thank You for using everything that happens to create good in our lives. Forgive us that we take so much for granted. When we are quarantined in our homes, cleanse our hearts and restore a righteous spirit within us. Change our lives so that we may start a revival that will change the lives of others.

Whatever we may be facing, build our faith and character so that we will follow Your paths, strong and capable of leading others. Bless the churches as they reach out to those that need to know You. Help us to rest and not worry about what lies ahead. You have already taken care of tomorrow. You hear our cries for help. In Jesus's name we pray. Amen.

Love, Grits

PS: Pray the hardest when it is hardest to pray.

Lent

What is Lent? Lent, in a Christian's life, is the six-week period before Easter—the celebration of the death and resurrection of Jesus. During this season, Christians examine their own lives and open their hearts to know God in a deeper and more intimate way. They observe and prepare for the celebration through intense prayer, fasting, meditation, and Bible study. Some Christians give up something meaningful for Lent while others focus on giving to those in need.

I think Lent should be a combination of the above. I think that the discipline of giving up something that is not healthy (like chocolate or Coke) is good for me. It reminds me that I can't have every pleasure I want. I feel I should also do something to help others, to take the time to do the things I need to do. Visit the lonely, clean my closet and donate the extra to the poor, volunteer in the soup kitchen—these are just a few of the possibilities.

Most importantly, I want to set aside more time for reading scripture and praying. I try to pray every day, but I intend to concentrate on praying hard and intensely for this fallen world and the many people suffering, scared, helpless, and homeless. I need to pray for those with no faith that they might find and know Jesus so they can receive God's grace.

I have so many blessings and have had so much joy in my life, and I have also been through many trials and troubles, but my faith in Jesus always sustains me. I pray that all can find a strong faith to help them get through the struggles of life. Lent is the perfect time to prepare for a deeper relationship with God and to reflect on Jesus and the cross and the resurrection while strengthening our faith and leading us to everlasting life.

Give it some thought and do something extra for God. Make every week of the year your own personal Lenten season, not just the six weeks of Lent. Kneel at bedtime and pray, read scripture, visit grandparents, call an old friend just to say "hello, I miss you." Pick up an extra can of food each week and put it in a donation box. Go the extra mile to serve others. Encourage your family to do the same.

> Is not this the kind of fasting I have chosen: to loose the chains of injustice, and untie the cords of the yoke, to set the oppressed free and break every yoke? Is it not to share your food with the hungry and to provide the poor wanderer with shelter—when you see the naked, to clothe him, and not to turn away from your own flesh and blood? (Isaiah 58: 6–7 NIV)

Dear Lord, help us to be totally unselfish during the Lenten season and all throughout the year. Help us to share Your love, care, and compassion with others. May we always be a blessing to someone each day. May we never forget the sacrifice You made for all of us on the cross, the beauty of Your resurrection, and the wonderful hope of everlasting life. Amen.

Love, Grits

PS: Footprints in the sand are not made while sitting down.

The Grandstands

Have you ever been a spectator at a track-and-field meet? Trust me, it's not a lot of fun. Long days lasting six to eight hours; events scattered everywhere, never knowing what time your event might take place; and then having to stay until the very end for awards.

I ran track in high school, and every Saturday during the season, my mom never missed a meet. She would pack our lunch, sit in the stands in the hot sun or pouring rain, and wait patiently for my events. She never complained. She was my support and my number one fan. She cheered when I won and gave me encouragement when I lost. When I needed rest, I could sit beside her in silence, her arm around my shoulders, and rest. Looking up and seeing her in the stands gave me strength and comfort.

I miss those days, and I miss her. I wish I could tell her how much I appreciated her being there. I'm sure I never told her back then.

Now God has taken her place in the grandstands. The grandstands of life. He is always there, patiently watching over us, encouraging us, picking us up when we fail, and cheering us on when we succeed. We often become so tired that we just need to sit by Him, feel His loving arms around us, and rest. When we are strong again, we continue on, always looking up and knowing He is there cheering us on. With Him on our side, we are able to successfully run this race of life.

> But those who hope in the LORD will renew their strength. They will soar on wings like eagles; they will run and not grow weary; they will walk and not be faint. (Isaiah 40:31 NIV)

Dear Lord, thank You for a wonderful mother who supported me in every way. I am thankful she is with You now and, I am sure, encouraging me still. I am so thankful that I have You on my side, and I pray I can always look up into the grandstands and You will be there. My Rock, my Encourager, my number one Fan. Amen.

Love, Grits

PS: Keep looking up; God is always looking down.

Pride

Pride deceives us into thinking we can do God's work without God's power.
Faith proves that only through God's power are we able to do God's work.

All things are possible through Christ who strengthens us. (Philippians 4:13 KJV)

Dear Lord, through our faith, work in our lives today. Show us the way. Take away our foolish pride and make us humble ourselves before You. Amen.

Love, Grits

Map Quest

MapQuest is a great tool for navigation while traveling. Punch a few buttons, put in the destination, and there it is, all laid out for us to follow.

God has provided a map for us also: the Bible. It is the greatest map of directions we will ever have. All the answers to all our questions are right there. Open it up, read some of its treasures, and you will be surprised at how clear things will become.

Thy word is a lamp unto my feet and a light unto my path. (Psalm 119:105 KJV)

Dear Lord, help us set our ultimate goal and destination on Your promise of everlasting life. Then help us move forward in the direction You are leading using the guidance of Your Word, the Bible. Amen.

Love, Grits

PS: Do not go where the path may lead; go instead where there is no path and leave a trail.

The Hunt

People often ask why I like going hunting. To be honest, it's not the hunt I enjoy as much as sitting deep in the woods, surrounded by trees and nature, away from the hustle and bustle of everyday life. A place so peaceful and quiet you can actually hear the leaves drop. I hear woodpeckers knocking rapidly on the nearby trees. I hear the flutter of the birds' wings as they glide from branch to branch. The hoots of the wise owls echo through the woods along with the sweet song of each tiny bird. Crickets chirp, frogs croak, and squirrels scurry around gathering acorns to bury for the winter months. I sometimes catch a quick glimpse of a rare fox squirrel.

I watch as the rays of sunlight glimmer through the trees and slowly dim as the sun sets at the end of the day. I just don't take the time to see and hear these things at home. It's a time to be still, watch, and listen. I have time to pray, rest, think, or just clear my mind. And if a deer shows up, it's a bonus. And my camera is always ready for a shot!

So to answer the question, it's not about the hunt. It's more about the peace I am searching for. It's a place I feel close to God through His awesome creation. It gives me an unexplainable peace and love for this beautiful display of nature. I may hear Him speak to my heart in a quiet way, or I may just feel His peace. Either way, I am blessed by each opportunity I get to sit in a deer stand.

Always take time to enjoy nature and the beauty around you. Find a place that is beautiful to you. It may be the beach, the river, a park, a waterfall, the rolling hills of the mountains, or even your own deck or backyard. Remember to be thankful not only for the creation, but for the Creator. But most important of all, find your place and take the time to feel the presence and peace God will give you there.

Let the heavens rejoice, let the earth be glad; let the sea resound, and all that is in it;
let the fields be jubilant, and everything in them. Then all the trees of the forest will sing
for joy; they will sing before the Lord, for he comes… (Psalm 96: 11–13 NIV)

Dear Lord, thank You for Your beautiful creation. Help us to realize what You have given us and remind us to take the time to enjoy it. Help us to feel Your presence and peace as You meet us there. Amen.

Love, Grits

PS: God's signature is all around you; learn to recognize the handwriting.

The Eighteen-Wheeler

My granddaughter and I left Charleston for a horse show in a small town upstate that I had never heard of. It was almost dark as we headed out, way later than we had planned. I did not want to tell her I was nervous driving at night to an unfamiliar location, so I just took a deep breath and said a little prayer as we headed on our way.

Just as I expected, she was asleep before we even got to the interstate. Trucks and cars were passing us like we were standing still. My palms were sweaty, and I considered just pulling over, but that really was not an option. I pulled in behind an eighteen-wheeler that seemed to be traveling at a reasonable speed, even though I knew he would probably soon leave me way behind.

As I looked up, I saw that the lights on the back of the truck made a perfect cross. I immediately felt my tensions ease. If only I could follow this truck to our exit. Miles went by, and the truck never left me. The cross was so clear, and I could feel God saying, *Follow Me, I've got this.*

For several hours, I drove completely at peace. As we got near our exit, I did not want to leave this beautiful cross and the peace it brought, but it was time. As we approached the exit, I couldn't believe it when he turned on his blinker too. I thought there was no chance he was getting off on the same exit as us in this remote area, but he did. I was so grateful. At the end of the ramp, I turned right and he turned left, never to be seen again. But never forgotten.

There was no doubt in my mind that God placed this truck in front of us to lead us safely to where we needed to be. We never know where or how God will lead us. He answers our prayers in ways we could never imagine. He takes our fears and worries and He takes control. Ask for His help. Look for His presence wherever you may be in whatever circumstance you are in. Never, in a million years, did I think God would lead me with a lighted cross on the back of an eighteen-wheeler. Oh, what an awesome God we serve!

> I will guide you along the best pathways for your life. I will advise you and will watch over you. (Psalm 32:8 NIV)

Dear Lord, never let us doubt that You are with us wherever we may be. Thank You for hearing our prayers for help and coming to our rescue. Amen.

Love, Grits

PS: It is nice to be important, but it is much more important to be nice.

PS: Tradition says that inside every sand dollar, five small doves form a perfect star representing the star of Bethlehem which shined down on Jesus the night He was born. I truly believe the untouched sand dollar was God's sign to us that He was watching over them and protecting them from this tornado.

The Sand Dollar

Milo, E, and the girls crouched together on the bathroom floor with their arms around each other and prayed. It was all they could do. The storm had come during the night, so fast and so furious. Their greatest fear, the tornado of September 2016, was upon them. Prayer was their only hope.

As they prayed, the trailer shook and felt like it was lifting off the ground. The sound of the wind and trees crashing around them was unbearable, and their fear was unimaginable. In a matter of minutes, it was over. It was eerily quiet and dark as they looked outside, still trembling with fear. No tree was left standing, the horses were gone—total devastation surrounded them. The girls called for help while Milo and E went to check on the neighbors.

Hours passed before anyone could reach them through all the debris and downed trees. But they were alive; their prayers, answered.

When daylight came, it looked like a war zone, but miracles were visible everywhere. Some of the neighbors' homes were completely destroyed, but at least they were alive. Their horses were found safe. Babe—an abandoned baby deer they had fed and cared for prior to the tornado, who should not have been able to survive the storm—walked up to the porch for his supper.

Tears of joy for the blessings in the midst of the devastation could not be held back. Then, they saw the sand dollar. This tiny single sand dollar that had been on the porch rail was still in the exact same position in perfect condition. It was then that they realized the amazing presence of God had been with them. Total devastation was around them, but their home remained standing, unharmed by any fallen trees. They were alive and safe, and the sand dollar was untouched.

I think of the story of Noah and how he and his family and the animals were loaded onto the ark before God closed the door. He protected them through the storm and the flooding and settled them safely on dry land again. God surrounded Noah and his family just as He surely surrounded my family that night.

Never underestimate the power of prayer and our God. He can be the miracle in the midst of any storm in your life.

The Lord is my rock, my fortress, and my deliverer; The Lord is my rock, in whom
I take refuge. (Psalm 18:2 NIV)

Dear Lord, I can never thank You enough for protecting my children in the middle of the storm. Please protect us all from the storms of life. Thank You for being there when we call for help. Be our Rock, our Fortress, and our Deliverer. Thank You, Lord. Thank You. Amen.

Love, Grits

This nation will remain the land of the free only so long as it is the home of the brave.
—Elmer Davis

Taps

"Day is done, gone the sun,
From the lake, from the hills, from the sky;
All is well, safely rest, God is nigh."

The sun is setting, the day almost gone. I sit quietly and watch as the sun slowly falls out of sight. I hear the laughter of a child in the distance and the song of the crickets around me. It's time to be thankful for the day, the blessings I see, and the many I do not.

Taps often comes to my mind as I watch the sun slowly set over the horizon. I think of my grandson who recently was fortunate enough to walk with his ninety-five-year-old great-granddad, a survivor of the bombing of Pearl Harbor, to the edge of the aircraft carrier Yorktown and throw a wreath in the water in memory of those who were killed at Pearl Harbor.

I know he is too young to realize the importance of the occasion and the honor he had in being with his great-granddad at this ceremony in recognition of these brave men and women who died while fighting for our freedom. Too young to recognize that his great-granddad, along with so many others, was a true hero.

His great-granddad has gone to be with the Lord now, but I intend to continue telling my grandchildren, and all children, the World War II stories my father told us so that the brave men and women who fought so hard for our freedom will never be forgotten.

We must keep history alive and pass it on to our children. We so often take our freedom for granted and forget that this freedom was hard-fought for with many, many lives lost along the way. These heroes deserve our sincere appreciation and respect. They deserve to have their stories told so the next generations will remember.

I see history fading away all over this country, but we must be diligent in passing on these valuable lessons. Remember it is only because of their service and sacrifice that we are able to enjoy the freedom we have now. There are very few heroes of World War II who are still alive today, so it is now up to us to preserve their history and sacrifices. May we never forget the dedication of our servicemen and all they continue to do for us every day.

Greater love has no man than this, that he lay down his life for another. (John 15:13 NIV)

Dear Lord, thank You for our freedom. Thank You for the servicemen that now serve and protect our country. Thank You for the brave heroes who have fought in the past, especially those who gave their lives for our freedom. May we never forget their sacrifice and be forever thankful for their service. Amen.

Love, Grits

Massa Jesus

A few years ago, I read the book *Candle in the Darkness* by Lynn Austin which took place during the time of the Civil War and slavery. Caroline was the daughter of a wealthy plantation owner, and Eli was a servant who was also her dear friend and almost like a second father.

The war had ended, and Caroline knew nothing would ever be the same. She did not know how she could face the future and began to doubt her faith. Reflecting back, Caroline remembered the wise words of her cherished friend Eli: "Faith don't come in a bushel basket. It come one step at a time. Decide to trus Massa Jesus for one little thing today, and fore you know it, you be puttin yo whole life in His hand."

As time passed, Caroline realized how true Eli's words were. She cherished his wisdom and friendship. She continued to pray. She told a friend, "God did not instantly reward me with a bushel basket of faith. But by the time I said amen, I felt strong enough to get through the day. I would have to pray every day, several times a day, but that was the only way to face all my problems…one day at a time"

Don't we all feel overwhelmed with life at times? We need to remember the words of Eli: one step at a time, trust Massa Jesus, and put your whole life in His hands. With prayer and faith, we can all face our problems, just as Caroline did; one day at a time, one prayer at a time.

Morning by morning, O Lord, You hear my voice. Morning by morning I lay my requests before You and wait in expectation. (Psalm 5:3 NIV)

Dear Lord, we are often faced with hard times, overwhelmed with no answers or direction. Please strengthen our prayer and our faith to put it all in Your hands and then to trust You with all our hearts. Thank You, Lord. Amen.

Love, Grits

PS: What lies behind us and what lies before us are tiny matters compared to what lies within us.

Sin

We are all sinners. We all make mistakes and will continue to make mistakes, but if we turn to God in prayer and repentance, He will completely forgive us. His whole purpose in dying on the cross was to forgive us of our sins. His last words were, "Father, forgive them, for they know not what they do." What a sacrifice He made for us. What a comfort to our souls.

We must continually make the effort to forgive others for the hurt and pain they may have caused us, just as He forgives us of our sins each day. Often the hardest part can be forgiving ourselves. Forgive freely as God forgives us. Forgive yourself. When we let the bitterness go, God will fill that empty space in our hearts with love and joy.

Go make peace with all: you will find a joy that only comes through God's forgiving grace.

As far as the East is from the West, so far hath He removed our transgressions from us. (Psalm 103:12 NIV)

Dear Lord, thank You for the gift of forgiveness. We continue to sin, and You continue to forgive us when we come to You in earnest prayer. Help us to be strong to fight off the temptations of sin and rely on You for strength and direction. Help us to forgive others as You have forgiven us, and help us forgive ourselves and receive your peace. Amen.

Love, Grits

PS: The greatest oak was once a little nut that held its ground.

Hopefully you will memorize these verses and let them be your strength and hope:

My rock:

Do not fear, for I am with you. Do not be dismayed, for I am your God. I will strengthen you and help you. I will uphold you with my righteous right hand." I memorized this verse and have repeated it over and over. It taught me not to fear. He is with me and He is my God. (Isaiah 41:10 NIV)

My assurance:

"Therefore I tell you, do not worry about your life, what you will eat or drink; or about your body, what you will wear… Look at the birds of the air; they do not sow or reap or store away in barns, and yet your heavenly Father feeds them. Are you not much more valuable than they? Who of you by worrying can add a single hour to his life?" The more I read this, the more I learn not to worry. My heavenly Father takes care of me. (Matthew 6:25–27 NIV)

My encouragement:

Do not be anxious about anything, but in everything, by prayer and petition, with thanksgiving, present your requests to God. And the peace of God which transcends all understanding, will guard your hearts and your minds in Christ Jesus. (Philippians 4:6–7 NIV)

My strength:

I can do all things through Christ who strengthens me. (Philippians 4:13 NIV)

My peace:

"…the Lord is my Shepherd, I shall not want. He maketh me to lie down in green pastures: He leadeth me beside the still waters, he restoreth my soul: He leadeth me in the paths of righteousness for His name's sake. Yea, though I walk through the valley of the shadow of death, I will fear no evil: for thou art with me; thy rod and thy staff they comfort me. Thou prepareth a table before me in the presence of mine enemies; thou anointest my head with oil; my cup runneth over. Surely goodness and mercy shall follow me all the days of my life: and I will dwell in the house of the Lord forever." (Psalm 23 KJV)

My hope:

And we know that in all things God works for the good of those who love Him, who have been called according to His purpose. (Romans 8:28 NIV)

Growing Faith

Life is not easy, and God's Word tells us to expect this. But every trial in life leads us to an opportunity to build our character and strength. During the trials I faced during the recession of 2009, I felt my faith and trust in God building. I would pray and read the Bible and search for comfort and answers. He always gave me peace and reminded me to hold on to my hope and keep trusting Him. I was so thankful. I felt good about my faith.

But trial after trial kept coming. How much more, Lord? How much more? As I continued to read and study the Bible, the words began to take on a deeper meaning. I was understanding more and more about what each verse was saying. My prayer time became my personal time with God.

Time after time, He took my fear and turned it into trust. The words were reaching deep within me, strengthening my inner soul, building a new level of faith and trust. I let the words speak to me and guide me. My prayers turned into conversations, not just requests or pleas—but God comforting me and leading me to a total trust without any doubts. He was building my faith upon a rock. He was teaching me to recognize His voice. I memorized many verses and fell back on them to strengthen me. Many are listed on the preceding page.

I no longer wake up in the middle of the night, anxious and sweating. Instead I remember my verses and feel peace. I picture myself climbing in His lap and resting with my head on His shoulders. On hard days at work, I say a quick prayer and smile in peace. Worry, fear, and anxiety have been replaced with peace and strength. And it all can be found in the Word of God.

For years I thought my faith was strong, but I have come to realize that was only the beginning of what God had planned for me. My story continues not without trials but with a renewed faith that can only be built through these trials and only with God's help. I will continue praying, reading my Bible, and memorizing verses. They hold me up when I become weak. God gives me a peace that I cannot understand and do not deserve.

And now we are in the biggest crisis of our time with the COVID-19 pandemic, economic uncertainty, riots, and nationwide division. I should be crazy scared, but I am not. I know my God is with me. Where my story goes from here, I don't know. I just know I am right where He wants me right now. Full of faith and hope, not seeing the future, but knowing He will take care of me.

There will continue to be trials of every kind, but we have a God who will continue to lead us. What an awesome God! Nothing can come between the love I have for Him and the love He has for me.

Dear Lord, thank You for the Bible—Your Holy Word—the place we can go to find instruction, comfort, and peace for our lives. Thank You for giving me hope when I felt there was no hope. I know life will continue to be full of trials, but I know You are right beside me leading me down the path You have chosen for me. Amen.

Love, Grits

PS: Don't pray when it rains if you don't pray when the sun shines.

Worship

      This early morning, the earth is a temple of light. You have given it to us, O God, and fresh in glory each day, You bid us bask in its wealth of life. In worship we drink in Your infinite strength and joy. My soul magnifies Your matchless grace and the beauty of Your holiness, yearning thus to clothe itself anew with garments of purity and truth. As the earth is bathed with the freshness of dew and light, so the purpose of God is for our souls. And my soul agrees! For pure as the light and free as the air and sweet as the lark song is the love of Christ, who made it all and walked the ways of earth in lowly sacrifice. Light and life and love are in all His ways, and still He walks among us. Him we worship in our souls' best thought and love, in the unity of the Father and the Holy Spirit. Amen!

      May we wake up each morning and bask in His light, clothe ourselves in purity and truth, and always find God's peace in all that surrounds us. May we be the light that leads others to the love of God through Jesus, His Son.

Love, Grits

Worship

I was so fortunate to have met a wonderful couple who were originally from Columbia, South Carolina, and lived in Charleston for a while; but then military life took them to Manchester, Washington—a town close to Seattle. They had purchased and read a copy of my first book, *Grits, God Reigns In The South,* and were coming back to Charleston to visit friends and wanted to have me sign their book. I was so honored that they even wanted to take the time to see me.

As soon as we met, I felt like I had known them for years. During this wonderful visit, we talked about the military, the places they had lived, our mutual friends, and how Charleston is so different from Washington State. A major difference they noticed was the lack of churches there compared to the many quaint churches of all kinds everywhere here in Charleston.

Seattle is a large growing city full of many young adults, but there are very few visible signs of religion there; very unlike what my friends were used to in South Carolina. They so enjoy visiting Charleston each year, the place they call home, and feeling the spirit of the Lord in the beauty of the Low Country and its churches and renewing the many cherished friendships they have here.

I was so saddened by the thought of this place with so little religion. I have always lived in a place so rich in faith. I cannot imagine Charleston without her beautiful steeples rising above the landscape. I cannot imagine not being surrounded by faithful caring people.

After talking with my friends, I was better able to understand the situation that is going on in the state of Washington and our entire country today with all of the riots, protests, unrest, and destruction. I now realize there are so many people in so many places who have no God and no faith in their lives. They are looking for a peace and hope that they will never find without God. They have never attended church or been given the opportunity to know the hope and joy that our faith gives us.

I can now appreciate how COVID-19 and social distancing have only strengthened our churches as they reach out to share the message of our Lord and Savior. I can also now understand how those with no faith or hope can turn to violence and destruction in search of a solution to their problems and concerns. I pray that God's message will reach some of those who do not know Him and give them peace and hope for a better future. I will pray hard for them. I do not know how to solve the problem, but I do know how to pray, and I will continue to pray for all who do not have the peace of God.

We all need to pray for all those who need to find the love of God and the hope, peace, and joy that He brings to all who will call on Him. Please help me in praying for all who need to find the Lord.

The grandfather of these special friends was the Reverend Martin Luther Banks, who served the Methodist Conference of South Carolina for more than sixty years. They shared with me a prayer he wrote that I would love to share:

Teach Your Children

I happened to overhear a conversation where a young mother asked another what camps she was sending her children to for the summer. The mother suggested a local Bible School that was very good. The other mother then stated, "I really don't want to send my son to a camp that teaches about God."

I was really shaken by the words and was very sad. I wanted so much to say something, but I was speechless. It made me realize that there are so many children today that do not know anything about God. It made me think of my Sunday School class that should be filled each week with happy children learning the stories of the Bible, but in reality, the numbers are few.

Children of this world need Jesus. We are living in a broken world that will do anything and everything to turn our children away from God. We must be diligent in teaching them at home, reading them the stories of Jesus, taking them to Sunday School, participating in Bible Schools, and saying prayers at dinner and bedtime.

We are so busy getting them to sports and school events and birthday parties that we simply are too tired to take time for Jesus. Children learn the most in their early childhood. We cannot wait, or else the world will teach them otherwise. If they are not strong and committed in their faith when they are young, they will turn and follow the ways of the world as they grow older.

Love your children, your grandchildren, your great-grandchildren, and their friends enough to give them the gift of faith that must come through your words and actions. Make time for this. This will probably be the most important lesson you will ever teach your children.

What we have seen God do for us, and what He has done for His people throughout history, must be passed on to the next generation. Their future depends on it. Teach your children well.

> These commandments I give you… Impress them on your children. Talk about them when you sit at home and when you walk along the road, when you lie down and when you get up… (Deuteronomy 6:6–7 NIV)

Dear Lord, let us never fall short in passing our faith onto the children. We must teach the children. If we do not, they will never know the hope of everlasting life. Amen.

Love, Grits

PS: The character of your children's tomorrow depends on what you put in their hearts today.

Train up a child in the way he should go: and when he is old, he will not depart from it. (Proverbs 22:6 NIV)

Love, Grits

PS: People may not remember what you say or what you do, but they will always remember how you made them feel.

Feeling Special

Every summer as a child, I looked forward to traveling the back roads of South Carolina to a small town called Olar. I went with my Aunt Sister to visit my grandparents and my other three aunts. "We're going up the country," we would always say as we began our journey.

We counted cows and church steeples, and sang songs, and the two-hour trip was over in no time. I will never forget sitting on the back porch of the old house shelling butter beans and snapping green beans. When we had a pan full, we would empty it into the huge pots my grandmomma had boiling on the old stove, preparing them for canning.

Pan after pan, we emptied into the pots. Sweltering heat did not stop my grandmomma from getting this done. It was their food for the winter. They had been through the Great Depression, and even though things were getting better, she would not take any chances. It was her way of life. To me, the fun and laughter that came along with the work and sweat was exciting. We would collect the eggs from the chicken coop, check the aging meat in the smokehouse, feed the animals, and ride in the back of my granddaddy's old pickup truck to the farm to check on the cotton and corn crops.

It was always so exciting and fun, and I knew at the end of the day there was always homemade ice cream in the churn. Near bedtime, my grandmomma would take me on her lap, open her china cabinet, and give me three shiny pennies for the next day. The first two pennies were for a bag of candy at the little country store, and the other penny was to put on the railroad tracks that ran behind the house. The train would run over and flatten the penny, and what a treasure that was to find it after the train passed.

On Sundays, we were always at the Baptist Church. I will never forget the loud preacher, who scared me a little, and the beautiful sound of "Rock of Ages," which we sang at the top of our lungs. Oh, how I love that song to this day. I still remember saying blessings before every meal and at bedtime, and how my grandmomma and aunts read me so many stories about Jesus and then sang songs around the piano.

Little things, but lifetime lessons I will never forget. I felt so special when I was around them, just spending good wholesome time together, but creating priceless memories that continue to influence my life today. They implanted in me a love of family and the seeds of my developing faith. I will always be thankful to them for their role in creating the strong faith that I have today.

It is so important to make children feel special. We never know when a memory we make with them in their early lives will make an impact on who they are, what they believe, or who they will become. Share your faith, your kindness, and your love with them. Share your time with them.

With God's help, when they are older, they will remember these special times you spent with them, your actions, what you said, and most of all, how you made them feel special. They may stray, but hopefully with God's help, they will remember the valuable lessons you taught them and turn to Him for help. I strayed for a while, but the values of all those who loved me, and the faith they shared, turned my life around and made a difference in who I am and what I believe to this day.

About the Author

Pam Morris Hanckel, Grits, was born in Charleston, South Carolina, the daughter of Princess and David "Buck" Morris. She grew up on Johns Island and spent every possible minute outside, in the woods, or on the river. One of her loves is offshore fishing, which led her to meet Miles, her husband of forty-six years. They have three children—Milo, Ryan, and Hope—and seven grandchildren—River, Addie, Emory, Ryan, Colin, Miles, and Sadie.

She is an active member of St John's Parish Church and teaches the children's Sunday School class. She is a former school teacher and now works at the family boat dealership. Her pride and joy are her children and grandchildren, and she loves fishing, crabbing, boating, kayaking, shark-teeth hunting, and playing outdoors with them. She was quoted saying, "I have always said saltwater runs through my veins. It runs through my children's veins, and I am now working on my grandchildren. I can think of nothing better to pass on to them, other than my faith."

Her love of God, His presence in nature, and her love of family and friends inspired her writings of faith and hope, in this book as well as her first book, *GRITS, God Reigns In The South*.

Pam would welcome your thoughts and comments about her book. Please feel free to contact her at phanckel@gmail.com.

CPSIA information can be obtained
at www.ICGtesting.com
Printed in the USA
LVHW072352250422
717217LV00020B/890

9 781638 441069